Social Media-Driven Travel Planning

Table of Contents

The real voyage of discovery consists not in
seeking new landscapes, but in having new eyes.

— Marcel Proust

Chapter 1. Introduction

Immerse yourself into the vibrant world of "Social Media-Driven Travel Planning" through our special report! Travel planning has leaped far beyond the traditional map and travel agency, moving into the exciting digital realm of social media. Are you curious about how Instagram is influencing our bucket list destinations? Intrigued about how Facebook recommendations shape our travel experiences? Eager to understand how tweets can guide our travel choices? Then this report is just for you! With insights from industry professionals, success stories from travelers, and hints and tips on how you too can harness the power of social media for your next adventure, our inviting yet substantially detailed report promises a journey like never before! Get ready to dive into the future of travel planning!

Chapter 2. The Evolution of Travel Planning: A Brief History

Our expedition into the past begins with an era when travel was purely functional, undertaken for survival or trade rather than for leisure. Journeys were arduous, long, and often perilous, reserved only for the brave souls willing to face the unpredictability of the wilderness. The only travel planning involved deciding on a destination and hoping for the best.

2.1. The Advent of Maps and Compass

With time, the era of exploration unfolded, turning travel into an exciting venture of discovering new lands. The creation of maps and the advent of the compass facilitated this process. Early travelers would painstakingly chart their routes, creating rough sketches on parchment that gradually evolved into more accurate representations. With these innovations, people could venture further into the unknown, with a somewhat increased level of certainty.

2.2. The Rise of Travel Literature

As more corners of the world were discovered and explored, travel literature started to emerge. Journals, memoirs, and letters of explorers became a window into unfamiliar lands for those who stayed behind. Notably, Marco Polo's accounts of his travel across Asia stirred curiosity and invoked a sense of wanderlust, setting the groundwork for travel as a leisure activity.

2.3. Birth of Modern Tourism Industry

The early 19th century witnessed the birth of the modern tourism industry with Thomas Cook, a British entrepreneur, credited as the pioneer. He organized rail trips within the UK and subsequently across Europe, marking the conception of package tours. These trips offered a convenient option for the expanding middle class that had begun to enjoy spare time for leisure. This ignited a significant shift in travel planning, specifically moving it from an individual task to a service provided by a travel agency.

2.4. Evolution of Travel Agencies

The 20th century marked the golden age of travel agencies. With the increasing affordability of flights and advent of faster means of travel, the world had become more accessible. Travel agencies began to specialize, providing packaged deals, including accommodation, car rentals, and guided tours. Brochures full of enticing images of exotic locations served as the primary travel planning tool, inspiring people to venture to distant lands.

2.5. The Dawn of Digital Age in Travel Planning

However, the turn of the 21st century challenged the hegemony of traditional travel agencies as the internet vastly changed the way we plan our travels. Websites like Expedia, Orbitz, and Priceline started offering flight, hotel, and rental car bookings, simultaneously providing customers with flexibility in planning their trips. The erstwhile dependency on travel agencies dwindled as online resources became more ubiquitous.

2.6. The Rise of Peer Reviews in Travel Planning

Along with the convenience of online bookings, came a crucial aspect of the digital revolution in travel planning – peer reviews. Websites such as TripAdvisor allowed users to share their experiences about hotels, restaurants, attractions, thus profoundly impacting the decision-making process of prospective travelers. For the first time in history, the traveler had access to mass amounts of practical information, experiences, recommendations, and even visual insights before embarking on a journey.

It is crucial to note how these significant transitions have shaped our contemporary ideas of travel planning over centuries. However, the evolution of travel planning is continuous, and while we have seen the rise of digital mediums, the current buzzword is 'social media.' As we progress further into the 21st century, we notice that platforms such as Instagram, Facebook, and Twitter are not only helping to inspire, but also plan and book our travels. Hence, this inexhaustible journey of evolution bridges us into our next segment that delves into understanding the 'New Age Traveler'.

Chapter 3. Understanding the New Age Traveler

The New Age traveler presents a fascinating study of changing perceptions and lifestyle norms, nudged along by the winds of globalization and technological advancements. Driven by the thirst for unique experiences, the desire to embrace different cultures, and a penchant for sharing, this contemporary globetrotter is reshaping tourism as we know it.

3.1. The Shift to Experiential Travel

The past decade has witnessed a noticeable shift from time-honored tourism, punctuated by fleeting visits to popular landmarks, to a more experiential form of travel wherein individuals seek authentic engagements with diverse cultures, landscapes, traditions, and cuisines. As we navigate deeper into the realm of new age travel, we observe an organic alignment toward personalized, immersive experiences. This trend can be attributed to the modern traveler's yearning for non-generic, transformative journeys that transcend the prescribed narratives of traditional tourism.

The experiential travel trend is anchored in the premise of 'living' the destination rather than just 'visiting' it. The new age travel enthusiast revels in experiences such as learning to cook an Italian dish from a native Nonna in a rural locale, volunteering in a wildlife conservation project in the heart of Africa, or partaking in a traditional tea ceremony in Japan.

Social media indulges and fuels these desires by providing inspiration, facilitating connections with service providers, and offering a platform for sharing these unique experiences with a global audience.

3.2. The Rise of Fear of Missing Out (FOMO)

Another fundamental aspect of new age travel culture is the phenomenon of FOMO - Fear of Missing Out. It denotes the anxiety that emerges from the fear that one might be missing exciting experiences that others are indulging in. Social media platforms, teeming with pictorial narratives of offbeat travel experiences, often crop the seeds of FOMO, thereby influencing travel behavior.

Because of the intrinsic link between social media, travel inspiration, and FOMO, more people are exploring uncharted territories and lesser-known experiences. Seeing a friend savoring a rare dish at a hidden gem of a bistro in Paris, or another capturing stunning sunset hues in a quaint village in Santorini, has provoked an infectious itch to experience these unique adventures first-hand.

3.3. Embracing Responsible Tourism

Reckless commercial tourism activities have wreaked havoc on many pristine environments worldwide. However, the new age traveler, who is socially-conscious and environmentally-attuned, is seeking to mitigate these damaging impacts by actively espousing sustainable and responsible tourism practices.

This fresh perspective is largely defined by the implementation of eco-friendly practices, support for local economies, and respect for indigenous communities' cultures and traditions. Aided by social media platforms which often act as influencers and information bridges, travelers are increasingly becoming privy to the urgency of transitioning to responsible tourism. In fact, many platforms actively host conversations around sustainable tourism, disseminating best practices and educating users on the relevance of traveling with an ecological conscience.

3.4. The Need for Personalization

The new age traveler relishes personalization. The 'one size fits all' model of tourism is giving way to bespoke travel experiences curated to cater to individual preferences. Thanks to the explosion of technology and data insights, travel-related businesses are better equipped than ever to offer tailor-made services, from custom-designed itineraries to personalized culinary experiences.

In addition, the new age traveler is heavily reliant on peer-to-peer reviews and recommendations. They seek guidance from fellow travelers on social media platforms to assist them in their decision-making process, leveraging their experiences to shape their own.

Conclusively, to understand the new age traveler is to acknowledge their quest for immersive, genuine experiences. It is to understand their voracious appetite for exploring lesser-known paths, their respect for the environment and local cultures, and their yearning for personalized journeys. Bereft of the traditional tourist's boundaries, these globetrotters are eschewing beaten paths to traverse the road less traveled. They are the resonant voice of a new era in travel, one that is footnoted in every tweet, Facebook post, Instagram caption, and Pinterest board.

Chapter 4. The Influence of Social Media on Global Travel Trends

Our examination of the mutual relationship between social media and global travel trends begins with recognizing the profound influence these interactive online platforms hold over our travel decision-making. They have become indispensable, serving as virtual travel guides, allowing real-time interactions and connectivity, catalyzing user-generated content, and gaining significance as potent channels to share, inspire, and effect travel plans and preferences of millions of users around the globe. The decisive shift from traditional travel methods to social-media driven travel is vital to understanding contemporary travel behavior.

4.1. The Role of inspiration in travel decision-making

Long before the advent of the internet, travelers relied on printed travel guides, word-of-mouth suggestions, and travel agencies for inspiration. Fast-forward to the digital age, various social media platforms are redefining how modern-day travelers seek travel inspiration.

The constant bombardment of magnificent landscapes, hidden gems, delectable local cuisine, and other varied dimensions of a destination captured artfully and shared by users instigates an irresistible urge to explore these facets personally. From these snapshots of moments in time, potential travelers weave a tapestry of dreams they hope to someday actualize.

Moreover, the dynamism of social media and instant access to user-generated content considerably reduces the gap between the desire for travel and its actual materialization. A study by Google found that 83% of people in the U.S. who use their mobiles for travel inspiration do so while in their daily routine.

4.2. The Revolution of Word-of-Mouth in Social Media Era

Cherry-picking destinations based on peer reviews and personal experiences has been a long-trusted strategy in travel planning. But with social media's meteoric rise, the conventional word-of-mouth has evolved into a digital and global phenomenon.

Independent travelers increasingly consider online reviews and recommendations. Review platforms like TripAdvisor, long Facebook threads about best places to visit, influencers' blog posts and tweets, and Instagram stories with geolocation all contribute to a more informed pre-travel phase. The shift towards digital word-of-mouth reflects in statistics too. In Nielsen's 'Global Trust in Advertising' report, it's stated that 83% of respondents somewhat or completely trust the recommendations of friends and family.

4.3. User-Generated Content: From Consumers to Creators

Social media, characterized by its user-centric nature, has propelled a shift from pure consumerism to content creation. Travelers have transformed from mere consumers of travel services and destination characteristics into creators of diverse travel-related content.

Platforms like Instagram, Facebook, and Twitter are brimming with engaging contents like photos, videos, and reviews, which are essential elements of the user-generated content model. User-generated content influences prospective travelers with authentic and persuasive narratives far beyond traditional advertising's reach.

4.4. Social Media Marketing: The New Age Advertising

The ubiquitous nature of social media has opened up avenues for firms, destinations, and travel services to engage in targeted advertising, reaching potential travelers at a fraction of the traditional marketing cost.

Using social media's precise data analytics, it's possible to isolate market segments based on their behavior, preferences, and demographic profiles. Advanced algorithms track user activity, enabling tailored advertisement strategies, thus augmenting reach and adding personal appeal to the marketing messages.

4.5. Social Media and Sustainable Travel

In the context of global travel trends, we cannot overlook social media's role in promoting sustainable travel. Promoting less-traveled destinations, Indigenous communities and their traditions, local gastronomy, or eco-friendly accommodations are ways in which social media users and influencers are advocating responsible travel. Such content not only cultivates a conscious breed of travelers but also equitably distributes the economic benefits of tourism.

4.6. The Dark Side of Social Media Influence: Over Tourism

While social media platforms offer numerous benefits in travel planning, they also hold a darker side. The popularity of certain destinations plastered across these platforms has led to oversaturation or 'overtourism.' It leaves negative impacts on the environment and local communities, portraying a side-effect of this social media-influenced global travel trend.

The fascinating interplay between social media and travel is an intriguing field of study, providing insights into the transition from traditional to digital travel planning. The myriad ways social media influences travel choices exhibit its transformational impact on global travel behavior. Understanding the complexities and potential of this dynamic will help us develop practices for more informed and sustainable travel planning. The aforementioned trends substantiate social media's role as a game-changer in shaping contemporary tourism discourse.

Chapter 5. Diving into Main Platforms: Instagram, Facebook, Twitter and Pinterest

As we delve into the universe of social media platforms, we must first examine the primary players in this grand digital theatre and their overarching influence on travel planning. Instagram, Facebook, Twitter, and Pinterest are at the forefront of this revolution, each platform wielding its unique influence on the eager globetrotter and suggesting tantalizing locations for them to traverse.

5.1. Understanding Instagram: A Picture is Worth a Thousand Recommendations

Within the seemingly infinite scroll of Instagram, travel enthusiasts have found a boundless source of inspiration. The visual nature of this platform verifies the age-old adage, "a picture is worth a thousand words." The striking aesthetics of a destination often pique the interest of users, encouraging them to further investigate the place tagged in the breathtaking image. It is this inherent curiosity sparked by visually compelling content that forms the backbone of Instagram's influential prowess in travel planning.

User-generated content, essentially photographs and videos created and shared by ordinary travelers, has exponentially increased the platform's reach. It enables prospective travelers to glimpse into the authentic experiences of others, thereby promoting trust and relatability, and influencing their travel decisions.

Moreover, the platform's algorithm curates a tailored feed for each user based on their interactions, pushing location-specific content that aligns with the user's travel interests. Thus, Instagram serves the dual purpose of inspiring and guiding travel enthusiasts through the minefield of travel planning.

5.2. Facebook: The Power of Social Recommendations

While Instagram nourishes the aesthetic appeal, Facebook leverages its community-driven design to influence travel choices. With the ability to make recommendations, review locations, and share experiences, Facebook presents its users with a digital trove of first-hand travel knowledge.

Travel communities and groups on Facebook foster a degree of trust due to the connection between users. Thus, a recommendation or a shared experience within these communities carries a lot of weight and can greatly influence a member's decision on a destination or specific travel experiences.

Moreover, Facebook's marketplace offers advertising opportunities to businesses in the travel sector, allowing them to present their offerings directly to interested users. It couples this with a comprehensive analytical tool that provides businesses with useful insights into user behavior and preferences, further aiding them in customizing their marketing endeavors.

5.3. Twitter: Travel Microblogs and Real-time Interactions

The Twitter platform offers a unique proposition – rapid and real-time communication. Travelers can tweet about their experiences, issues, or insights as they occur, providing immediate and often candid understandings into a variety of travel scenarios.

Hashtags can prove an invaluable tool for compiling information and providing access to diverse content from many users. For example, a simple search for #ParisTravel might yield a myriad of user experiences, hotel recommendations, culinary delights, and must-visit attractions, providing a broad view of what to expect in Paris.

Also, Twitter serves as a real-time news platform where users can get updates on location-specific events or situations, such as weather conditions, political unrest, or cultural events. It empowers users to be well-informed and make swift travel decisions.

5.4. Pinterest: A Vision Board for Travel

Pinterest operates as a digital vision board, enabling users to identify their travel interests and aspirations visually. Users pin images or information from across the internet onto thematic boards. A "European Vacation" board, for instance, could carry images of scenic locales, links to informative blogs, posts about local cuisine, and more.

The platform's Save button encourages users to add pins from any travel related website onto their board. These pins often lead users to external websites, making it a useful tool for businesses such as travel agencies and resort chains to drive traffic and build a robust online presence.

Pinterest's unique ability to categorize and visually lay out trip specifics aids travel planning. A prospective traveler can arrange their list of preferred sights, attractions, accommodations, and even create a week-by-week or day-by-day itinerary, effectively making Pinterest a guidebook customized to each user's unique interests.

5.5. Tying the Threads Together

Each of these platforms holds a unique role in the panorama of social media-driven travel planning. Instagram's visual allure, Facebook's social recommendations, Twitter's real-time communication, and Pinterest's vision board design blend together to create a comprehensive and readily accessible network of travel information and inspiration. As digital natives become the prime explorers of this world, understanding these platforms can transform the way we plan our journeys, making the process more personalized, dynamic, and engaging. As we forge ahead, the symbiosis between social media and travel seems destined to strengthen, leading us to new frontiers in the realm of travel planning.

Chapter 6. How Instagram Inspires Globetrotters

The magic of Instagram lies in its persuasive power and visual allure. Embedding this dynamic into the heart of travel planning has led to a seismic shift in how journeys are conceptualized, planned, and undertaken. Expansive landscapes, exotic cultures, mouth-watering cuisines, represented through impactful images and engaging videos on Instagram are redefining the travel industry. This chapter aims to decipher the multifaceted relationship between Instagram and globetrotters - a relationship underpinned by inspiration, manipulation, and growing ambitions of capturing the perfect 'Instagrammable' moment.

6.1. Visual Storytelling and the Desire for Authentic Experiences

The essence of travel lies in experiencing the new, the unknown, the spontaneous. But now, much of that spontaneity has been predisposed by the narrative we see on Instagram from travel bloggers, influencers, and even our very own friends. They weave a visual tapestry of locations, blurring the lines between a personal diary and a global showcase of the world's hidden and known gems. These visuals create a domino effect, engendering a form of vicarious satisfaction and a relentless yearning to experience the same - a phenomenon recognized as 'Instagram-induced wanderlust'.

From catching a sunrise on a picturesque mountain top to indulging in local delicacies in vibrant city markets, Instagram has made globetrotters privy to a kaleidoscope of travel experiences. People are not just looking for destinations; they're seeking authentic experiences - the local life, the cultural immersion, the unique interactions - that travel bloggers habitually broadcast through their

Instagram stories or posts, consequently shaping travel trends and desires.

6.2. The Rise of Instagrammable Travel

In conjunction with the desire for authentic experiences, the aspiration to capture that perfect 'Instagrammable' moment and validate one's travel experiences through 'likes' and comments has been on the rise. This trend has compelled many globetrotters to preplan their trips, basing their travel choices on how admirable a location may look on their feeds, or how likely it is to evoke envy, admiration, or wanderlust in their followers.

This pursuit has also led to a measurable impact on local industries, tourism boards, and the hospitality sector at large. Recognizing the value of this metric, many destinations and hotels have started marketing themselves as 'Instagrammable', going as far as creating 'Instagram spots' or 'photo points', designed primarily to match the aesthetic expectations of the Instagram-user. This phenomenon has played an instrumental role in driving tourism and contributing to the growth of numerous local economies worldwide.

6.3. Travel Hashtags and Discovery

Hashtags on Instagram have become one of the most potent tools for travel discovery. By following or exploring certain tags, travelers can delve into the depth of unexplored destinations or learn about popular travel spots. Among the most used, hashtags like #Travel, #Wanderlust, #Travelgram, #InstaTravel, lead users to millions of travel-related posts, thereby creating a trove of information and inspiration.

In addition, Instagram's 'Explore page' algorithmically suggests posts based on users' past activity, interests, and location, etc., opening up a world of new travel inspiration. This disrupting feature integrates globetrotters into a giant, intertwined network of travel enthusiasts, granting them access to diverse, unfiltered travel content.

6.4. Instagram and Sustainable Travel

On the flip side, Instagram has been under scrutiny for promoting 'over-tourism', ultimately harming local ecosystems or cultures. This has led to the rise of another sub-movement within the Instagram travel community– promoting sustainable travel behaviors and destinations.

Influencers and ordinary travelers are starting to showcase more sustainable ways to travel and experience cultures, minimizing their footprint, and focusing on activities like supporting local economies, choosing eco-friendly accommodations, and exploring less-touristic areas. Hashtags like #EcoTravel, #SustainableTravel, and #ResponsibleTravel are increasingly coming into play.

In conclusion, Instagram's influence on travel planning and experiences is colossal and multifaceted. From inspiring globetrotters with visual narratives and experiences, driving them towards capturing Instagrammable moments, helping them discover new destinations through hashtags, and more recently, steering them towards more responsible travel behaviors, Instagram has staged itself as a critical catalyst in shaping the definition and scope of modern-day travel. This 'new-age' travel, propelled by social media, represents a dynamic blend of exploratory desires and digital maneuvers, the scale of which we are only beginning to comprehend.

Chapter 7. Facebook Recommendations: Laying the Groundwork for Personalized Travel

In the new-age digital realm of travel planning, Facebook has etched a prominent presence, owing to its personalization capabilities. Unrolling the carpet to a world of travel recommendations, Facebook forms the basis of a significant number of travel plans across the globe. Armed with the insights from Facebook friends and the platform's intricate algorithms, many travelers are concocting customized, unique, and unforgettable travel experiences.

7.1. The Power of Recommendations

Facebook recommendations harbor the power to be truly transformative in the landscape of travel planning. When a user posts a query for travel advice on their feed, friends and family members respond with thoughts, ideas, and experiences. This organic form of positioning travel recommendations enables explorers to gain access to a wealth of knowledge and personal experiences that guide books and general internet research might miss.

But it's not just the word-of-mouth endorsements that boost travel planning. The inherent structure of Facebook facilitates the collation and preservation of these travel recommendations. Unlike fleeting conversations, these suggestions remain retrievable for future reference. This persistent storage makes a visible and constantly accessible repository of travel wisdom tailored for the individual, building a foundation for the next great adventure.

7.2. Algorithmic Personalization and Travel Planning

Personalization thrives at the heart of Facebook. The platform's underlying algorithm curates the information seen by each user, based on their past activity, preferences, and engagements. This extends to the realm of travel planning as well.

Ads from travel organizations, suggestions for travel-related groups, and posts from pages offering travel services - all are strategically placed on our feed. It's like having a virtual travel agent who knows your preferences intimately. By noting the types of posts users react to and the sort of travel content they share, Facebook assists them in discovering new destinations, inspiring future travel plans.

7.3. Case Study: Harnessing Facebook Recommendations for Personalized Travel

To illustrate the incredible potency of Facebook in shaping travel experiences, consider the story of Julie, an ardent traveler. Julie sought to explore the offbeat path on her next journey —something distinct from popular travel guides. She posted her specific needs on her Facebook feed, sparking a flurry of recommendations from her network. Through these responses, punctuated by recommendations for local eateries, niche museums, and hidden hiking trails, Julie designed an unparalleled, personalized travel plan.

Facebook's algorithms didn't miss the chance to engage as well. Along with friends' suggestions, they served ads for local accommodation and transport services, easing Julie's logistical worries. Here, Facebook recommendations formed the basis of a unique and memorable travel experience, highlighting the platform's power in travel planning.

7.4. The Future Scope of Facebook Recommendations in Travel Planning

As much as Facebook has revolutionized contemporary travel planning, it holds a promise of even more growth. Travelers are increasingly gravitating towards hyper-personalized experiences, and Facebook's algorithm shows immense potential for catering to these preferences.

Furthermore, Facebook's recent evolution into a marketplace for goods and services provides an excellent opportunity for direct interaction between travel businesses and potential consumers. This pushes the boundaries of simple recommendations, opening the door for seamless travel booking experiences. Imagine not only discovering a unique destination through Facebook but also booking accommodations, local transport, and experience packages all within the same platform.

7.5. Leveraging Facebook for Your Personalized Travel Planning

As a savvy traveler ready to embark on your next adventure, understanding how to harness Facebook's power is crucial. Here are a few tips:

- Actively engage with travel-related content to train the Facebook algorithm to show you relevant suggestions.

- Join travel-related groups on Facebook for more diverse suggestions and real experiences.

- Don't hesitate to post your travel queries on your feed, tapping into the collective wisdom of your social network.

- While planning, use Facebook's saved items feature to store useful recommendations for easy access.

In conclusion, Facebook reshapes how we approach traveling. With a blend of organic and algorithm-based recommendations, it lays groundwork for uniquely personalized travel experiences. As the platform continues to evolve, this influence on travel planning is set to deepen further. Being cognizant of this can empower us to sculpt truly remarkable and personalized travel plans.

Chapter 8. Twitter and Travel: Microblogging Our Way Around the World

In the era of digital nomads and tech-savvy travelers, Twitter has emerged as more than just a microblogging platform; it's a global travel companion, allowing explorers, young and old, to chart and share their adventures around the world. Daily, millions of tweets run through the veins of Twitter, providing real-time updates, travel anecdotes, and invaluable insights into a myriad of global destinations.

8.1. Tackling Travel Planning with Twitter

Twitter, in its exquisite simplicity and immediacy, becomes an accessible tool for travelers. By following the right accounts, users can quickly track flight deals, spot opportunities, and stay updated on regional events that might shape their travel experiences. Airlines, travel ventures, official tourism boards, and seasoned adventurers curate a never-ending stream of 280-character pulses, creating an ecosystem that fuels wanderlust and rewards curiosity. Users can take advantage of relevant hashtags such as #TravelDeals, #TravelAdvice, or #TravelTuesday, allowing them to dive into an ocean of travel intel, right at their fingertips.

8.2. The Whistle-Stop Tour: Twitter Threads

Twitter also introduces a unique storytelling format, the thread, that has found prodigious use in travel narration. Users document their journeys 'tweet by tweet', stringing along a series of posts that come together to form the virtual equivalent of a travelogue. These character-limited narratives weave together diverse fragments - from candid moments and charming local cuisine to priceless interactions with locals and awe-inspiring snaps. A well-crafted Twitter thread can transport the reader right into the heart of the traveler's journey, blurring the lines between virtual observation and physical existence.

8.3. Real-time Interactions: Striking Gold for Travelers

The real-time nature of Twitter can help travelers solve travel predicaments, with airlines and tourism boards actively maintaining their handles to address travel-related grievances. A well-timed tweet can swiftly elevate your problem to the masses' eyes, often leading to swift action and problem resolution. Moreover, live-tweeting can intensify the thrill of sharing real-time travel experiences, allowing the excitement of exploration to spread like a digital wave over the platform.

8.4. The Power of Twitter Chats

Twitter chats are yet another marvel of the platform, acting as a nexus for like-minded travelers seeking interactive discourse on travel-related topics. These scheduled sessions follow a format where a host (usually a travel influencer or agency) announces a topic and time, prompting followers to join the conversation using a specific hashtag. The result is a vibrant, rapid-fire discussion, interspersing travel advice, shared experiences, and helpful suggestions, offering an enriched collective wisdom to all participants.

8.5. Case Studies: Successes of Twitter in Travel Realms

While all of these instances epitomize the platform's utility for travelers, let's review some of the best cases where Twitter shone as a travel companion. User @SarahExplores, for instance, learned of a rare aurora borealis sighting in Iceland through Twitter, allowing her to witness this once-in-a-lifetime spectacle. Twitter's real-time nature proved invaluable for @TravelsWithTed when an unexpected storm caused a series of flight cancellations. He was able to find an alternate route after spotting a tweet from an airline offering extra seats on a different flight.

8.6. Using Twitter to Enhance Your Travel Experience: Best Practices

To wrap up, let's go through an array of best practices to use Twitter to its fullest potential as a travel tool. Following official tourism accounts and airlines gives you quick access to updates and deals. Make sure to engage with the community by participating in Twitter chats; they are a goldmine of tips and advice. Tweet with relevant hashtags to share your experiences and find others. And don't forget to embrace the Twitter thread – a perfect way to document your journey and trace your digital footsteps across the globe. Take advantage of this vibrant platform and let Twitter guide you around the world, 280 characters at a time.

The ever-evolving landscape of social media holds intrigue and promise for the future of travel planning. Twitter has emerged as a key player, offering travelers a uniquely interactive platform to navigate their journeys. Microblog away, fellow nomads - a world of global wisdom and shared experiences await on Twitter!

Chapter 9. Social Media and Tourism Industry: A Symbiotic Relationship

Embracing the digital age, Tourism and Social media have combined to forge what can be aptly described as a mutually beneficial relationship — a symbiosis— which we now explore in-depth within this chapter.

9.1. The Mechanics of the Marriage

At its core, the link between social media and tourism is intimacy. The former, an ever-evolving platform for interaction, allows strangers to become virtual neighbors. Meanwhile, tourism, a venture typically subjected to sterile brochures and remote agencies, has gained personalized and immediate touch through social media. The favor is returned as tourism content offers social media users an escape from the mundane, introducing them to new horizons just clicks away.

Social platforms like Facebook, Instagram, Twitter, and Pinterest have rapidly become integral parts of the travel experience, from the initial planning phase to the sharing of experiences post-trip. Tourists increasingly turn to these mediums to narrate their travel stories, piquing others' interests, and setting off a cycle of aspiration, planning, experience, and sharing, further invigorating the social media-tourism loop.

9.2. Role of Social Media in Tourism Industry

Social media has opened a dynamic communication and marketing channel for tourism providers. Tour operators, airlines, hotels, and other stakeholders use these platforms to promote their products and services, receive feedback, resolve issues, and build lasting customer relationships. The constant exchange between service providers and consumers has led to the democratization of the tourism industry, where customer reviews are as powerful as promotional content, if not more.

This interactive relationship between the tourism industry and potential travelers via social media platforms has also allowed for the cultivation of a much-personalized travel experience. Tailored tour packages, customized services, and precise recommendations are now possible through data mining and analysis of the users' activity on social media platforms.

Case in point, Facebook targeted advertisements or Instagram's 'Inspire Me' feature are just manifestations of advanced algorithms that read and learn from customer's preferences depicted through their social media interactions. The result is a win-win situation with businesses maximizing customer satisfaction, and customers receiving bespoke travel experiences.

9.3. The Boon of User-Generated Content

The tales of travel narrated by people on social media platforms are an invaluable resource for the tourism industry. User-generated content (UGC) works as authentic, trusted peer-to-peer marketing, to which potential travelers attach more credence than traditional forms of advertising. Furthermore, these shared stories give insight into real experiences, helping service providers better understand market behavior and adjust their offerings accordingly.

Travelers are not just consumers but also creators of content. Photos, reviews, and blogs shared on social media channels help create narrative and visual maps of destinations, influencing others' decisions while driving publicity for visited locales. The virality potential of a picturesque snap on Instagram or a rave review on Facebook should not be underestimated in its capacity to sway potential travelers.

9.4. Social Media and Sustainable Tourism

As social media become the stage for exposing both the enticing and ugly side of tourism, it plays a dynamic role in shaping sustainable tourism practices. Social media users have been vocal about various issues such as overcrowding, environmental degradation, and socio-cultural disruption, encouraging the industry to be more accountable and tourists to be more responsible.

Platforms like Twitter have often triggered and accelerated discussions on such topics, leading to positive changes in the industry. On the flip side, trends on Instagram or Pinterest foster positive practices like eco-friendly travel, cultural immersion, and locally sourced experiences. Here, social media acts as a catalyst for change while educating its users and influencing next-gen travel habits.

9.5. The Challenges Ahead

Like all relationships, this symbiosis also has its share of challenges. Misinformation and 'photoshopped' expectations can promote unsustainable tourism practices. Issues of data privacy and the authenticity of online reviews also demand attention. However, the power to transform these challenges into opportunities rests within thoughtful navigation of the social media landscape by both the industry and consumers.

In conclusion, the interplay between social media and the tourism industry is characterized by reciprocity and co-evolution, where one feeds into and grows with the other. Through social media, the tourism industry is not only transformed but also empowered to influence, showing us that when warm beaches and winter cabins meet tweets and tags, the outcome is a journey that is as exciting as the destination itself. As we move forward, this relationship will continue to mature, offering new avenues for exploration. As is the essence of travel, it's not just about reaching the destination but also about the path taken to get there.

Chapter 10. Future Predictions: The Next Era of Social Media in Travel Planning

With the ceaseless advancements in technology and the avid embrace of social media by the contemporary traveler, it is undeniable that the landscape of travel planning is swiftly moving towards a more digitalized future. Much like the prodigious embrace of the internet in the 21st century, the next era of travel planning is surmised to be just as transformative, if not more, with the burgeoning reliance on social media platforms.

10.1. The Rise of Augmented and Virtual Reality

The ever-evolving technologies of Augmented Reality (AR) and Virtual Reality (VR) are shaping the next era of social media in travel planning. Imagine scrolling through your Instagram feed, falling upon an awe-inspiring image of the Aurora Borealis, and being able to virtually stand under this natural light display, feeling the thrill of the cool air, or hearing the gentle rustling of leaves in the background. All this before even booking a ticket. This is the immersive experience that AR and VR are expected to bring to social media, providing travelers with a uniquely captivating preview of their potential destinations. Companies like Google are already starting to incorporate AR into maps, providing real-world directions overlaid on your phone camera view.

The incorporation of AR and VR technologies is also predicted to revolutionize travel content created by influencers. The capability to share immersive experiences can further enhance the allure of their content, influencing more people to plan their journeys based on these virtual experiences.

10.2. The Emergence of AI-Powered Recommendations

Artificial Intelligence (AI) is another force to reckon with in the realm of social media-driven travel planning. As social media platforms gather tonnes of data about user preferences, AI can help analyze this data to give tailor-made suggestions. AI can infer users' potential interest in certain destinations or experiences based on their past behavior, hence refining the travel planning experience for each individual user.

Furthermore, with advancements such as AI chatbots, travel companies can provide real-time assistance and answer querents immediately, revolutionizing customer service in the travel industry. These digital assistants can also offer personalized travel recommendations, acting as virtual travel agents on social media platforms.

10.3. Enhanced Authentic Experiences Through Live Streaming

Live streaming on social media platforms can provide a real-time view into the destination's environment, culture, and experiences, self-empowering individuals to make informed travel decisions. It's one thing to see a static image of a bustling market in Morocco, and another to watch, live, as vendors display rich, vibrant arrays of spices, and locals haggle for the best price. This kind of interactive media cannot only help travelers prepare for their trip but also shape their expectation realistically.

10.4. Rise of Social eCommerce and Instant Booking

Lastly, the integration of eCommerce in social media platforms is exceedingly likely to mould the future of travel planning. 'Book Now' options are becoming progressively common on social media platforms, allowing users to transition from discovery to booking seamlessly. The convenience of this feature could result in a higher conversion rate, shifting the entire travel planning experience to social media platforms entirely.

In conclusion, the future of social media in travel planning is set to be dominated by AR/VR, AI-powered recommendations, live streaming, and social eCommerce. It is thus evident that as technology evolves, so does the way we plan our travels. As we continue navigating this shifting landscape, one thing remains certain: the integration of social media in our travel planning is here to stay. It will redefine the lens through which we view our future travel endeavors, marrying the thrill of spontaneity with the efficiency of technology and the immersive, explorative experience of travel.

Chapter 11. Your Guide to Leverage Social Media for Travel Planning: Best Practices and Tips

With the digital revolution and rise of social media, travel planning as we know it has been dramatically reshaped. The immense potential it possesses to guide, inspire, and personalize your travels is a frontier waiting to be explored. Now, embark on this exciting venture, armed with a plethora of strategies, best practices, and tips to effectively utilize social media for your future adventures.

11.1. Embracing the Social Media Platforms

Putting all your travel planning eggs in one social media basket is not recommended. Each platform, whether it's Instagram, Facebook, Twitter, or Pinterest, brings its unique flavor, and fully tapping into their capabilities can provide a well-rounded and rich travel experience.

Instagram feeds are peppered with stunning locales inviting you to luxuriate in the beauty of diverse landscapes. It's an excellent platform to visually explore potentially under-the-radar destinations from all corners of the globe. Furthermore, geotags and location-based tagging can lead you straight to these beautiful spots; a simple click reveals a treasure of related images and experiences shared by other travelers.

Facebook presents a more personal approach. Leveraging the platform's recommendation feature, tips, and reviews posted by your friends, or based on your preferences, can provide insightful and trustworthy first-hand information about various destinations.

Twitter, on the other hand, with its real-time updates, offers a micro-window into the world. It's particularly useful during the trip planning stage, as you can track weather updates, live situations, and recent reports from various locations around the globe.

Pinterest is your gateway to a scrapbook of ideas. From curated travel itineraries to unique local dishes you must try, Pinterest is an extensive archive of travel-based content that you can use as a reference during your planning.

11.2. Using the Hashtag Tool

Hashtags have been a game-changer in streamlining and navigating through the deluge of posts, images, and information present on social media. Using them effectively represents a crucial element to social media-savvy travel planning.

General travel hashtags like #travel or #wanderlust give you access to a sea of global travel content. Destination-specific hashtags, such as #VisitParis or #LoveNYC can provide city- or country-specific posts that reveal hidden gems, popular tourist spots, and local specialties. Don't forget to follow local tourism bureau or agency handles; these often curate well-researched, targeted, and useful travel content.

Also, explore unique, thematic hashtags, like #foodtravels or #solotravel, which can finetune your search based on specific interests or the type of journey you're planning.

11.3. Engaging with Influencers and Travel Communities

Travel influencers and bloggers promote a myriad of destinations and share their experiences, which can be a gold mine of travel planning information. Engage with their content; 'follow' them; ask questions; the interactive nature of social media platforms aids you in these endeavors.

Communities and groups on platforms like Facebook, Reddit, or travel-specific platforms such as TripAdvisor, can introduce you to a world of fellow travelers and enthusiasts. Here, real experiences, advice, discussions, and recommendations are shared freely and can influence your travel planning significantly.

11.4. Making Use of Travel Apps and Plug-ins

Many tech companies are jumping aboard the travel planning bandwagon, launching dedicated travel advice apps and plug-ins. Social media travel accounts, such as TripAdvisor, Airbnb or Lonely Planet, offer a wide range of services, from bookings and discounts to reviews and recommendations, all aimed at easing your travel planning process. Make sure you follow or subscribe to these handles to keep your travel planning strategies updated and invigorated.

11.5. Being Mindful of Social Media Pitfalls

While social media can inspire, it can also mislead. Glorified, or overly-filtered travel experiences might not depict the reality of a destination. It's prudent to use social media as an aid rather than the sole source of your travel plans, combining it with traditional sources of information like travel guides or local tourism websites.

Ultimately, the goal of your travel planning should be to create a journey that is truly your own – flavored by your unique tastes, preferences, and experiences. Once armed with the knowledge of how best to leverage social media's tools and potentials, you're all set to dive into this rich and infinitely inspiring arena of travel planning that awaits you.